sundry

a book of poems

sundry

a book of poems

by

kirsten sikora

Sextant Publishing,
An imprint of Cambridge Strategies Inc.
www.cambridgestrategies.com

First Edition

Canadian Cataloguing in Publication Data
National Library of Canada cataloguing in Publication

Sikora, Kirsten (1980 -)
Sundry

ISBN 0-9731134-3-X

1. Poetry
I. Title.

Editor: Stacey Sankey
Publisher: Ken Chapman
Design: Stacey Sankey
Cover Image: Kirsten Sikora
Author photo: Kirsten Sikora

Published by Sextant Publishing, an imprint of Cambridge Strategies Inc.
www.cambridgestrategies.com/sextant/sextant.htm

Cambridge Strategies Inc.
Suite 208 Empire Building
10080 Jasper Avenue
Edmonton, AB T5J 1V9
www.cambridgestrategies.com

The gift

When I came I was broken
There was nothing to believe in
Much less myself
And the gift they gave
Was not in gold
Nor any treasure
But in belief
They made the stars seem not so far away
The world a little less bleak
I woke up one day and realized
I had the power to silence my demons
And this is the kind of debt it takes a life time to repay
Thank you seems inappropriate
But they don't seem to ask for much

This book is dedicated to :

Wallis, Sandra and Glenna from the iHuman Youth Society; they encouraged me and helped me find my voice.

Brandi, Kendra, Dean, Nancy, Mohan and Steven -- my friends, who helped me whenever I needed it; whether is was typing, driving, feedback or support, they were there.

Stacey and Ken from Cambridge Strategies who decided to take a risk on me.

And most importantly, my mom, who...

1. *Always believed in me*
2. *Never gave up on me*
3. *Spent long nights awake worrying about me*
4. *Helped me to laugh in the face of many obstacles*
5. *Held out enough hope for both of us*

~Kirsten~

Forward

This book of poems emerges from a conversation I had with John Mould, Alberta's Advocate for Children and Youth. He was asking me to think about ways to "reconnect" Alberta's most vulnerable citizens, our youth-at-risk, with 'every day citizens' to ensure these children and youth become a higher priority for everyone.

My initial impression, and it's one I think most are guilty of, is that the average adult believes the government and the social agencies are enough. So long as 'these kids' are not stealing my car, breaking into my house or beating up *my* kid, and I pay my taxes, I have no further responsibilities, right? But I quickly realized that this kind of thinking just confirmed John's concern. There is very little chance for the mainstream to really connect with such challenged, challenging and sometimes frightening kids. There is little opportunity for most of us to even have a meaningful, truly helpful conversation with these youth, and even less opportunity to gain a better understanding of who they are. So we warehouse them or write them off and let them go to waste. We rarely, if ever, ask ourselves "what would it take to make a difference and if I tried to connect, what do I risk?"

Not long after my conversation with John, I began work on a project with Edmonton artists Wallis Kendal and Sandra Bromley. Coincidentally or not, these two were also the founders of the iHuman Youth Society, an arts mentorship program which operates for and by Edmonton's street kids. My association with them would provide a personal answer to the question "how do I connect?" While my 'natural tendencies' in dealing with these kids would fall into a traditional, hectoring, lecturing and disciplinary father function -- not particularly helpful in finding out who they are, what their gift is or how they might be helped -- the connection I was able to make, thanks to iHuman, was through these kids' self-expression in all forms of art and writings. The creative work they do in art, music, drama, dance and writing has been a chance to find common ground between 'them' and 'me.', a chance for me to better understand their human experience. This is a long way from making a difference but it is a start.

Kirsten Sikora has been one of those street kids and her poetry is but one of her gifts, (check out the cover art of this book for another example). She is a personal success-in-the- making…her journey is not yet complete but she is well on her way. This volume of her work is an experiment. It is intended to beg the question; "Can art and self expression be the bridge which will allow troubled youth to be better understood by the rest of us?" As you encounter her perspectives and experiences, be open to your insights and ideas. And, just as I was asked to do, consider how you, as a citizen, can become engaged in a common cause to help our vulnerable and at-risk young citizens. We have to do better.

Ken Chapman
Edmonton, Alberta
May, 2005

Table of Contents

I came here to tell you
Everything gets worse
It's up to you to make it worth it
Nobody else will give you a satisfactory answer
So suck it up and play your hand as best you can
When you give up you lose anyway
Me...I'm counting my dead who knows I forgot how to cry
I held your hand but I couldn't help you up
We are all drowning in selves we never get to really know
Someone once told me...
I loved you with everything I had at the time but it wasn't enough
And I know it will never be and I'm better for it
But none of what I say matters without ears to hear or eyes to see
Of which you had none
Life was like summer re-runs with new commercials; hopeless
Never knew what you'd see if you turned off the set.

Moths

I have always thought that
Maybe I burn
And through this smoke
I can't see anything clear
Maybe I light the way
but I'll consume whoever tries to hold me
Maybe moths alone
Brave the bright

This is a man I passed by on the way to the store, for whom the mirror still lies.

This is a woman selling herself for a moment's relief.

This is a baby born prematurely, unable to satisfy the craving his mother couldn't deny.

This is my father, who did whatever he could to find an excuse.

This is my sister whom society failed.

This is my best friend who can't see or hear anymore.

This is my first love that I can never let go of.

This is me.

Lessons

I know it now
I feel it in my bones
The paint
Funny, its quality is independent
Of taste
I see this woman,
A teacher
She could be mine
But I won't take her class
I want her to see
What I can do
Independent of her lesson
You see I've had my own lessons
They are written all over my hands
In my sideways glance
The curve of my lip

You are a fool but
But even you can see that

The girl you want is here
but you're gone now
                    fingerprints

I was always loosing things as a child
Books scarves mitts toys friends
Something's never change

Diamond girl

Diamond girl
Sparkle and shine
Harder than anything
I cut through your densest metals
Yet your sharpest edges
Don't even scratch my surface
My possibilities are endless
I seem impossibly strong
That alone is your grounds for
Seeing/Exploring/Pushing
So recklessly to the breaking point of
My centre
And when I shatter
You shake you head and walk away.

Eyes flick downward
As something glib and cynical
Rolls off my tongue
Onto the floor
Cringing, as I hear my own laughter
Hard
Sharp
Eyes flutter upwards
Lips pursed in a tight half smile
A grimace
I wonder if this is the same face
That once had cheeks sore from smiling
Endlessly wide
Eyes stare straight
Before falling flat
Glancing inward at the wreckage of self
Where bitterness and spite has collected, caked
Upon the joy that was once
So bright

Addiction two

Before the shot I'm aware. Brain sensitive as antennae. Every thing begins to hurt. I feel cold but I'm dripping with sweat. The rush comes finally. There are a few moments, when nothing could possibly be wrong. This is of course the time when things go permanently wrong.

Now let the countdown begin. Languid at first, letting the relief of my high wash over me. Faster, as I have to begin to seek anew, because there is never enough. The moment my heart stops it will be the end. I know only this truth. In some ways I have always known.

This is a story a very sad story

about a stupid little girl
who couldn't manage even the most basic ideas
Lace Cap

she had so many ideas about the way things
might be
but she couldn't put the pieces together
when it broke apart she didn't give up
not our girl
she kept at it, trying harder each time
any fool could see it wasn't meant to be
but she continued until her hands froze
and her whole self shook, and her mind
sputtered and back fired like an old car
Even still she tried to find the solution
'til her heart gave out from the weight
of disappointment
Lovely lavender
Goodbye

Addiction three

This is my mother

Standing over me

Her tears washing my face

But her eyes they aren't sad

They're worried

She has given up on me

Know that worry harbors hope

She won't ever give me up

The baby she fought hard for

But never knew

Or maybe that's a lie too

Maybe she always knew what I was up against

Maybe that's why she fought so hard

To love me

And make me feel it

So my darkness wouldn't be so alone

***

This is my best friend

Washing my arms

Trying to tell me it will be alright

But we both know it won't

As it's prophesied in the railroad tracks

Running up and down my body

As she spreads the cloth across my bruised legs

She wonders how far apart we must have been

For her not to notice sooner

That I was drowning

Now it's too late with my body submerged in

Soap, sweat, and both our tears

***

This is my sister

Calling out to me from the shore

I dove out too far and she can't see me

Endlessly her voice carries on the waves

I hear her body hit the water

Terror finally finds me

I try to tell her "no"

The waves are too high

The storm too violent

Water fills my mouth

Water which is drifting me

Farther from shore

Farther from her

I fight not to save her

Simply so she won't be alone

Stuck

I am immobile
Stagnant
Stuck on the inside
Due to faulty construction
I cannot be repaired
The wires are all mixed up
Connecting me to just one path
I am pulled inexorably to my end
But a good artist always finishes
And no work is ever truly complete
Thus I end where I began
Full circle to meaningless
No pills will placate me
This time round
I know not to even bother
No smooth words will comfort me
I bend and contort them
You see my last defense
Will kill me

Depression is like a demon in my mind
He waits for me
Never really leaves
Just sits at the edge of my thoughts
Ever patient
He's been there as long as I can remember
My imaginary friend with super powers
He can't control my thoughts
But he can bend them real nice
With the help of his minions
Fear and doubt
He loves my apathy
And my sensitivity
Because every time my heart wrenches open a bit
He gets closer to me
Sends his minions
To squeeze me
So I can't breathe
Then to my rescue he comes
And in his grip I remain
Until anger decides to bail my ass once more

After you were gone

After you were gone
The nights were long
The boys came out like rats in the dark
They tore and bit at my flesh
Taking the pieces they liked with them

Love

The word unfolds from my tongue
Only to be caught with my teeth and bottom lip
I wonder if this has anything to do with its nature
Does it spill forth from me and then I seek to capture it
Hold it inside
Maybe that's just me
Perhaps some pronounce it "luv"
The mouth slowly offering it
Like a kiss
I've seen some mouths sneer slightly
Like the word dirties them
Certain lips smile when they say it
While others frown
This most slippery of words
It seems to get away from all of us
For even though it's the most over used word
Our lips giving it every second of every day
We still feel a lack
L... O... V... E...
Nothing in its construction belies its meaning
Yet, that's the same with all words
Say something often enough it becomes empty

Meaningless

Going under

I am going under
So sick of watching this cycle repeat itself
Mutilated by your love
Counting all my previous scars
I'm in pretty rough shape
These feelings I speak of are not romantic notions
Just love simplified

I held my reserve steadfast
I was not going to let you come back
But your lips persuaded me
Without words
I feel weak
To what end
I ask myself

As tiny kisses of increasing passion
Unlace the binding of my heart
We share
An urgency that is born of
Disappointment
Loneliness
And unrelenting self-preservation
We are not lovers
We are not friends
We are generals of opposing armies
Fighting a war that has no victor
Only
Momentary conquests
And courtesies

For a Buoy

I saw you
Sensed a spark from the first
Something secret, sacred, soft
Soft
Like your baby-wide smile
That disarms me completely
Sucks the strength from my sadness
While your eyes
So bright, vivid, alive
Send joy-filled laughter bubbles
From my belly to my throat
Tickling my heart, pushing the corners of my mouth
Such is the beauty of your soft spark
I cannot bear to touch you
Why run my hands over your skin?
When it's the quality of your dreams I want to feel
Caress your hopes
Kiss your imagination
Spend all afternoon making love to your
Soft spark

See it in movies
Read it in novels and poems
Learn it in songs
This Love
This impossibly great thing
That we long/reach/push/fight/wait for
Yet when 'It' comes
We don't recognize that is really it
We expect a great love
Will come complete with
Large unmistakable signs
This will let us know
This is the love of movies, books and songs
We have found it
We are here
Our current love is a test run
A training ground to prepare us
For that one
  Perfect
    Love

Telegram

You're not here
Wake, sleep, feed
Breathe. Breathe.
Stop.

Laugh, Smile, Play
Sigh, Sigh,
Stop.

Dream, Panic, cry
Choke, Choke, Stop
Stop.

Begin again,

Monochrome

All these lovers I've had
without love
Their faces blurred in my vision
like a smear of paint
All the colours between Red and Blue
where I went down,
looking for you
Thinking foolishly, you'd be there
When I finally found the perfect hue

So I explored Indigo
Experimented with Magenta
Became addicted to Dioxazine
Infatuated with Amethyst
Only to submit to Lilac
Right before falling head over heels for Violet

All this searching did nothing
but leave me tainted,
tinted
and running back to Blue

Selfish

You never ask how I'm doing

I could be
Dying slowly
  from a wound
Caused years ago
Opened fresh
Bleeding out
Every time I see your face

But you never even wonder

Drifting away from you
Wanted so much
To plant roots
And grow strong
But instead
I am beach wood
Tossing around in the waves
Still lost on dry land

Emotionally dead?

You never gave me a
single
    thought
    tear
    not one real smile
Just emptiness and a plea
"Don't give up on me"
So I became a spy
Seeking to infiltrate your heart
Discover the secrets under your skin
And found you under mine
        Could you love me, under the skin?
        Or will I freeze here
        Waiting for you
I let go of you
And the hope that you can forgive me
I tried so hard to answer that plea
Don't give up on me

The first
thought
I had was that
You, you were gone and
Maybe you had never
been
Was it only in my mind
Maybe you never heard the
Rain
Tapping on the roof
Arms encircling
Unity of two
Against a storm that will not
Bend
You would never bend
It was always left to me to find
another way
to worry
to cry
to say goodbye
and mean it
so
is it any wonder
I wonder
that you may have never even
been
from the first thought

Fickle

Why can't my heart stay put
The feelings I have today
are not the same tomorrow
Forever moving
I don't look at you the same way
First you were a life raft
Then a playmate
Now somehow
You feel less
I want you back
So I think I can change it
Bring you closer
But maybe I'm just fighting the tide

Pity Empathy compassion
All that I have for you
You might never read these words
Doubt you'd even want to
I'd like to think
I could have made it better
Could have changed something
For you

But I am still invisible
You hardly see me
But I know you can feel me
In the languid night
Previously chilled
When we give what
We can
Reservations in the morning
saved

You Came

You came on
one of my good days
I cried anyway
Didn't seem to bother you

You came on
So strong
Wanting so much
Out of the blue

You came on
My belly
My throat
And my hair

You came on
A Saturday
And left town on a Sunday
So suddenly I shouldn't think on you again

I hope her snatch
eats you alive
I hope she has nothing
But pain in her breast
I hope your lying mouth
Rots on her skin
I hope it kills you
This fatal wound you've inflicted
Is nothing but a scratch
Just a scratch

Intoxicated

So much want!
I want this for you
That for me
Something for her

But I am empty
I see you, so much spark
Becoming intoxicated
By your movements,
I think
  If only...
But the things I want for you
Are not enough
Merely my silliness
In thinking I could change
Anything
So if I let you go
It's not at all like
Giving up
Merely letting go
To allow you
To become whatever
You choose too
As I watch
Intoxicated

Stepping into an alley,
the words are everywhere.
Some are sprayed on
others carefully typeset on little signs.
Some are scribbled hastily in jiffy marker.
the words penetrate my heart before they can float up to my rationalizing brain,
the blood surges to my eyes,
clouding my vision
and all at once it seems like the words are at war.
I have the sense that some are screaming, shooting
Some are simply groaning,
While others are whimpering in corners.
There are a few that boom their existence,
a couple that favor repetition as a way of being heard.
I am overwhelmed as I clap my hands over my ears, squeeze my eyes shut!
When I open them again
I am alone.
Nothing
But words and rain on stone.
I walk away.

What kind of hate breeds?

What kind of hate breeds?
A woman is walking to her car
It is late
Two men approach
Ask her for a cigarette
She pauses
They throw her into the back of a white van
They hurt her
Deep
The kind of hurt you don't
Ever heal
They hurt
They hate
The woman was snow
They burning red earth
The war is old
The hate they bore
Is born upon them
And all their relations
None of it is right
None of it makes sense
But when hurt is buried so deep
It blinds you to all but the pain

We are all trying too hard to be artists

We spend so much energy convincing everybody that
    We're the real thing
We are pretending

Our work shows who we are
We wait for inspiration to find us
    As though some muse would embrace us
    Take our pain, our isolation, our anonymity
    And replace it with brilliance

But if she's coming
She's taking her sweet time

So we idle our days in small cafes
    Sipping coffee as we read about the lucky ones

    The ones who don't wait
    The ones who sold us this bullshit artist schtick
    The tragic assholes whose tragic pose we are forever
    Emulating

    Fuck Van Gogh
    Fuck Cobain
    Fuck Pollack
    Fuck Morisson
    Fuck Plath
    Fuck Hendrix

    Fuck every suicide, every overdose, every crazed
    rampage, every lost soul, every died too young
    Every too good for this world, every famous tragedy,
    Every sensational tragedy, every goddamn martyr for
    This very marketable lie we've been buying into
    For the last 200 years

Morning Coffee

The words came
Pounding
but when I sit to express
I find my mind slow
Castrated
My body moving
With underwater difficulty
I try not to take it seriously
Parlaying despair with
The thought that
I am just percolating

I have this nagging suspicion
That God is a marketing exec
Named Steven
Trying to sell us on
Faith, love, marriage
Picket fences + paradise after
The devil is heading a rival company
Pushing drugs, isolation, violence
A fast car and a ticket to nowhere

In the end neither cares
So long as you are buying

Summer storm

A girl
Of striking beauty
Sure of tongue
Sure of fist

Like rain

Sometimes soft
   Soothing
Sometimes violent
Could make a rain
Bow

Low,
Terminal cancer of the mind
Degraded

The beggar is not permitted to shine
The brat is pretending to be something
The play's the thing
But it has fallen away from us
Claim the talent and took the dignity
I am too tired to fight
The time has flown
We must submit to something not our own
The delicacy of ownership
Possession is 9/10 of law
Now little bird
You are anointed
You are chosen
To say goodbye

Voicemail

There is no wall to block this storm
My skin is thin and open to the elements
Tiny comments ravage me
So I dare not talk to anyone
I am loved
I know that
                    My phone rings
                    from morning to midnight
                    with far away voices telling me
But I know what's coming
One by one
They will let go of me
Let me drown
Now I know that I have such a short time
Before this light goes out
               The snow is blowing in scattered directions
And if I move
My thoughts fly just as wild
My friends leave with the birds
Move south before
The winter fall
While I struggle against the fading of light
No hope of winning
Just too simply survive the cold
Once more
To emerge
Reborn
To die some other day

Sometimes, I ache for you
All of a sudden
I want to be 4 years old
Going to the kitty cat store
My hand in yours
You taking the time
To teach me
How not to backwash in my orange pop
I was about five when I realized
That we were different,
Although, not quite in opposition
We had a funny relationship
And now I realize
I was lucky to have anything at all

Temper Temper

Slapped across the face
by you're helping hand
Your good intentions
Murder me
Careless tongues sting
Leaving a throbbing ache
And a bitter taste
The lean so cruel to the fat
Unforgiving
I hope when your face
is a mess of wrinkles
And loose hanging flesh
My un-creased skin
Will have the compassion to spare you
The rough edge of truth

Looking over this place
Where we made our lives from paint
Now covered in generations of Jiffy marker
Where eloquence and idiocy mingle
With desperation and expression
Something you said once spies up at me
And I find myself staring hard at the space
Where you used to be

When we were fierce

Once upon a time
We weren't afraid of anything
Holes in our elbows and knees
Dirt under our nails
Homeless, Restless, Aimless
An extensive wardrobe of adventure

Let me tell you a secret

There is no pot of gold
There are no heroes

Not all mothers love their children
And lots of daddies just aren't there

Drugs can be the breast milk you never got
And violence can be your best friend

But the well is poisoned
And the last one you should trust; is the one who wants it the most

Nobody ever gets better
And we all die alone

Eulogies are designed to blow smoke up your rotting ass
And most kids cry on their birthday

Every war is killing somebody's baby
But they're just as invisible as the ones asking for change

Nobody cares about anything but themselves

Except you
Right at this moment
And if you hold onto that
There's hope

How to tell my story...
And in what context?

I have experienced enough drama to create and show a six part mini series. Or, instead, I could write a succinct ‘timeline’ version of my life -- the kind I needed to produce every time I saw a new Therapist/Psychiatrist/Social Worker.

I could start by telling you that I was born in Edmonton, AB, a place where, if flowers are going to grow they have to be hearty. Still, it pays to remember that despite the cold winters and dry conditions, wildflowers can be found in alleyways and sidewalk cracks. The people here grow like that too -- irrepressible.

I could paint you a stereotypical portrait of an angry, tough teenage street kid, but that wasn’t really me. At 14, I was more like a paper boat on the North Saskatchewan, perilous and fragile. I slipped through all the cracks, was tossed by the waves and still somehow miraculously managed to dock one day.

Or, instead, I could shock you, revealing how I lost my mind and subsequently became a heroin addict.

I could try to explain how all these events led to my landing at iHuman, whereby I discovered my passion for art and, with their help, salvaged my life and fashioned it into something I had never believed possible.

But...

...what I really want you to know is the journey through these experiences has taught me compassion and understanding.

...what I really want to tell you is, this is me -- within these pages, 24 years old now, still growing, exploring, and discovering.